I0839064

A World without Ivory

Poetry
By
Julie A. Dickson

Copyright 2018
Julie A. Dickson

All rights reserved

May not be copied
without permission
from the author

Dedicated to Nosey

and to all captive elephants

In circuses and zoos

who dream of freedom;

and to those humans

that advocate for

elephants and seek

to send them all

to sanctuary

A World without Ivory

Dye rhino horns and elephant tusks pink,
as humans attempt to protect, think of ways
to save land mammals, for slaughter reaches
a grand scale, that quest for ivory appeals
to some for riches and reveals human greed in
their darkest hour, as man continues to exceed
and dismiss warnings of extinction, will not
heed or give way to nature, in her methods
to cull or evolve, each species to survive.

Can humans even attempt to revive or solve
this dilemma while faced with men on the sea,
who brutally sever fins, release sharks to death,
so that chefs may create soup?

Caged primates in signs, speak to men,
hearing lies, taught to them - a language
they cannot believe, left to perish
by humans who cajole and deceive.

And humans berate and chastise- hate
a lonely captive killer whale who missed his family,
preferred not to play their games,
no longer wanted to entertain.

Solitary elephants in zoos, on cold concrete, stand
swaying, unable to speak or express sorrow -
man seems not to understand, that given land to roam,
not wrenched from family units, wander together,
ponder the next succulent branch.

The odor of burning ivory permeates, does not change the fate
of fallen beasts but some nations pass laws to cease the
trade.

Since poachers have killed for the largest tusks,
in Africa, some are born without –
genetic path or evolution, nature's way to decrease worth
and therefore survive? Though at what cost as they mourn
all who were lost at the hands of man…

Perhaps elephants dream of a world without ivory.

Five Willows Literary Review 2017
Avocet Nature Poetry Journal 2018

Plight

Gray sky over sparse trees,
gray skin stretched over
skeletons of strength,
lumbering stance
frames enhanced.

Trunks raised in alert,
rumbling underfoot,
herd encircles young,
matriarch searches,
surveys horizon.

Lone infant cries,
herd dispersed,
stands over carcass,
horrific mutilated
mother silent.

Instinct

Fly in perfect V formation
How do they know their destination?
With predetermined concentration,
Geese fly

The quest a longer sense of time
The gray beasts follow from behind
Continue in their single line
Elephants return

The current harsh but swim they may
Orange flashing bodies flip in spray
Jump and propel, they know the way
Salmon spawn

Animals with instincts known,
Purpose clear, the beasts have shown
Ears listen, scents as wind has blown,
Animals know

Humans cannot comprehend
Instead they seek out land, defend
Power sought, from the foes they fend
Man's folly

The Harvard Press 2014
The Avocet Nature Poetry Journal 2015

Elephants on the Plains

Standing in the red backdrop of rusty hills
Sketched crimson against the sands of time
The scarlet hues caressing dew kissed leaves

Tree limbs bathed in rejuvenating warmth
Elephants browse in majesty on the plains
Old and young feeding in the early morning

Sounds clear in dawn of day, quietly beckon
Crickets and tree frogs greet the morning
Birds announce the feast of awakened insects

Low rumblings, the trembling ground echoes
Footsteps placed solidly against the earth
Still water ripples in the wake of a breeze

Trumpets in reply to low voices calling out
Waiting patiently, calf follows to drink deeply
Choosing tender branches alongside her dam

Branches bent low as her trunk extends to grasp
The herd is restless in the open terrain
Ears flapping in signal; the matriarch warns

As one, they thunder away from oncoming threat
The dust cloud rises up from the road beyond
Stark metal rumblings carry the beasts called man

The Avocet Nature Poetry Weekly 2013
The Harvard Press 2014
The Avocet Nature Poetry Weekly 2015

Never Forget

They pulled me away from my sister
as she reached for me, her chains
stretched and rattled as she screamed.

Hands guided me into a truck.
I could hear but not see and I cried,
terrified- I stood still as we rode.

I never saw my sister as time passed.
I thought of her when they beat me,
when I did tricks and ran the ring.

At night, I dreamed she was there
beside me, as we leaned together,
bearing our loneliness.

Even that would have been better
than my solitude, in a trailer
not knowing where I traveled.

Each time they coax me forward,
Tugging at me with their stick,
I think I hear my sister.

So long ago when I cried,
she screamed out to me;
never forget.

Action Required

Attached firmly to the entrails
of receding justice,
we stand in shock, aghast.

Can the torch of Liberty burn out
so easily, extinguished by apathy,
or will we intervene?

Must it be the fate of humanity
to erupt into civil war,
knowing historically, they failed to resolve?

By voicing our truth, interpretive words,
dismissing silence as passive acceptance,
action required; peace is not attained by chance.

Good Fat Poetry Zine 2017
Five Willows Literary Review 2017

Ellie Tells

What is it like to be an elephant?

To watch your mother slaughtered,
To be wrenched from your family,
To be beaten and tied into submission,
To be sent to a stark, cold place alone.

What is it like to be in a Zoo?

To stand in a small enclosure, on concrete,
To never see another elephant,
To hear human laughter and screams,
To never forget your dying mother's face.

What is it like to go to Sanctuary?

To remember pain, attempt to heal,
To forage among trees, swim in ponds,
To hear the voices of your new herd,
To be allowed to be an elephant.

Bad Decisions

When nature's bounty is forsaken
how will humanity survive?
Could it be that we're mistaken
not to protect what is alive?

From the smallest insect, bumble bee
to mighty elephant , killer whale,
our population makes them flee;
no habitat, the species fail.

Human arrogance and waste,
destructive mechanization rules;
bad decisions made in haste,
How can mankind be so cruel?

The sea and earth we desecrate.
Can we stop the downhill roll;
save all beauty nature creates
before mistakes will take their toll?

Sways

Legs thick as tree trunks on concrete stand
Wonder how freedom might feel
Gray beast sways in sorrow

Prolific Press 3 Line Poetry 2018

Human Impact

Swelling hearts that feel remorse,
but enough to change our course?

Souls borrowed from eternity,
it takes a while for us to be,

To come of age, emerge the man
but we cannot understand

The impact of our words, our deeds,
the course of action without heed

Damaged waters, oil and waste
cannot replace the earth with space!

Inspired, search out to the stars -
we cannot live on Mars!

The greatest beasts, so close to man,
feel and reason, still we plan

Apes that communicate by hand
but we cannot understand

We hold them captive, experiment
sitting back, we ne'r lament

Humans boast the smartest brain
but then refuse to bear the blame

Motions set to right the wrong,
but the impact has been strong

The trees, in tragic falls lay down
leave behind a barren ground

Elephants have family ties,
man exacerbates the lies

For amusement, gray forms sway
in dire solitude, they pay

For humans to gawk and stare
most of us are unaware

Imprisonment does them no harm,
the emcee speaks with practiced charm

The dolphin shows, the squeals of glee,
captive mammals want to flee

Stolen young, they bear the scars,
trained response to flailing arms

When did man become so blithe,
with carte blanche to take a life

Intelligence to equal man's own,
to rob a species of their home

We truly need to grow and change,
question thoughts, to rearrange

Superior? How man believes,
the attitude, how we deceive

ourselves, our children need to learn -
our time on earth, it should be earned

Elephants

Elegant in their stance

Lumbering slowly through the forest

Echoed voices, rumbles as they feed

Patiently caring for their families

Handsome young bulls growing to adulthood

Aunts and cousins nurturing their calves

No death goes un-mourned among them

Tenuous grip on freedom slips away

Slaughter remains the imminent threat

Elephant Rug

[This was an innocent gift from my grandmother]

I received a large box by mail at the door.
Contained a strange pink and gray elephant
rug which was laid on my bedroom floor;
my grandmother's gift left me reticent.

My eyes widened with surprised dismay;
for on the high-polished floor by my bed
lay the thing, a seemingly innocent gray
strange oval rug with an elephant head.

The elephant rug was to stay in my room;
mother announced as she stood with me there;
I felt my heart fill with a sense of gloom
as those elephant eyes seemed to stare.

Routinely tucked into bed with a hug,
cocooned myself tightly within the sheet -
I dreamed of that terrible elephant rug,
convinced that I heard a real heartbeat.

The dream-elephant rose up, pink ears wide,
long trunk extended past black marble eyes;
and even though I had no place to hide,
sheets were protection that I devised.

Awoke in the morning, my mother appeared,
alarmed at the absence of the elephant rug
recalling my dream, those eyes I had feared;
rug locked in my closet, I gave her a shrug.

Diameter of a Tear Drop

Down my cheek rolls a single tear,
diameter of which remains unclear
lasting only a moment, not large in my eyes
but it's plain and this pain I fear
contradicts its minute size.

From an overhung branch will fall
a raindrop, I glance up to call out -
it's like a flood, one might think,
but its diameter is not much at all,
scarcely a taste, not enough to drink.

There are places where a puddle seems gold
even though they've often been told -
wait for fresh – tainted pool may cause them ill;
they drink water to abate a need that's grown old,
diameter of thirst grown past all free will.

Then a pond comes into view
and though clear waters might renew,
cleanse as a tear refreshes my eyes,
restricted diameter-available to few,
its purity savored only by rich and wise?

Lies a barren sea, expanse is wide
such diameter, impossible to hide;
collective pain, given no choice -
empty, no water found, they must abide
a sea of tear drops, silent voice.

Little did I Know

On Saturdays as a child
my father often took me to the zoo;
bought a warm bag of peanuts
in the shell and we sat on a bench.
Two elephants stood swaying
in an outdoor enclosure,
trunks snuffling the cement
floor for remnants of hay.

From between huge iron bars,
if I stood nearby, I felt warm air
expelled from the trunk
that I wanted to touch.
Back then we could feed them;
my father placed a peanut
on my small hand and pushed
my arm toward the bars.

Soon the small legume
was gently taken from me,
just the tip of the trunk
tickling my hand.
Years later when I read
about Lulu's death at 40
and poor Lil-E who died
even younger, I cried.

My love of elephants
led me to learn of zoo
life and circus torture.
I starting speaking up.
I still remember Lulu's
gentle trunk nibbling
a peanut from my hand;
little did I know.

Chain Free

There are those who truly live in chains,
great sentient beasts chained in misery;
echoed voices joined in so much pain,
women bound- dream an option to be free.

Some of us are chained by our own hand,
feeling trapped, but where to turn?
Forces from within make their demand,
and if we hold the key, we've yet to learn.

Captive elephants chained, cannot move
look to rescue, some to sanctuary -
with great effort, some battle to remove
sisters from their chains in empathy.

Cannot compare to those who cannot flee,
at least for us, perhaps we hold the key.

Elephants in Sanctuary

Old leathery façade all but hid the warm hearts,
swaying in unison, the gray pair stood touching,
almost embracing, two old elephants -
trunks intermittently entwined, reassured each other.

Ears alert, waving off small gnats that pester,
ankles scarred from the memory of chains not forgotten,
years to trust the creatures that only confused,
bringing food and hay, yet also pain of hook and sticks,
uncertainly waiting in fear, dignity all but vanquished.

Their majesty of size was no help to them then;
they were larger but were diminished into
loneliness and solitude.

Those scars served to remind of long years captive, alone.
In the vast depths of their souls, they suffered,
enduring the cruelness of those they had trusted -
beaten when unhappy, for defending their pride.

The long wait for rescue, final sanctuary in old age,
now in solitude, the freedom painfully earned -
beneath the sun, among trees and grass,
lying down in deliciously muddy ponds,
walking in unison, the elephant friends
will remember the past together.

About the Author

Julie A. Dickson is a New Hampshire Poet and Writer.
She lives with two rescued black cats and has always loved elephants.
Julie is a member of the Poetry Society of NH, The Portsmouth Poet Laureate Project and Writers in the Round at Star Island. Her works has been published in The Harvard Press, Five Willows Literary Review, The Avocet Nature Poetry Journal, Poetry Quarterly, Kind of a Hurricane Press, The Portsmouth Herald, among others. She has several published works of poetry, non-fiction, young adult fiction and children's books, available on Amazon.

About the Artist

Doug Vermette is a New Hampshire artist and amateur carpenter who enjoys gardening and home brewing

Save Nosey Now, Inc. is pleased to present the poems of poet and author Julie Dickson to aid in the fight to save captive elephants from their lives of torture and distress.

Dickson's candid prose clearly illustrates the circumstances that surround elephants in captivity but also holds promise of that better future in sanctuary.

Working together, people from all walks of life can make the difference in an elephant's life. We hope these poems touch your heart like they have ours and that their message stays with you long after you've read them.

Captive elephants deserve independence and freedom of choice. Join us in the fight for them.

Barbara Lovett

President

Save Nosey Now, Inc.

Please support Sanctuaries and Organizations

<u>United States</u>

ERNA
Elephant Refuge North America
Founder/CEO- Carol Buckley
Attapulgus, Georgia
https://elephantaidinternational.org/projects/elephant-refuge-north-america/

EST
Elephant Sanctuary of Tennessee
Hohenwald, Tennessee
https://www.elephants.com/

FOZE
Free the Oregon Zoo Elephants
PO Box 15239
Portland, OR 97293
https://www.freetheelephants.org/about-foze/

PAWS
Performing Animal Welfare Society
Ed Stewart
San Andreas, California
https://www.pawsweb.org/meet_elephants.html

SAVE NOSEY NOW
The mission of SAVE NOSEY NOW, INC. is to provide education, intervention, and litigation that will ultimately lead to sanctuary for captive elephants in circuses and zoos.
https://savenoseynow.org/

Please support Sanctuaries and Organizations

<u>International</u>

EAI
Elephant Aid International
Chain Free means Pain Free
Founder/CEO Carol Buckley
https://elephantaidinternational.org/

GSE
Global Sanctuary for Elephants
Scott Blais
Chapada dos Guimarães, Brazil
https://globalelephants.org/

BLES
Boon Lott's Elephant Sanctuary
Katherine Connor
Sukhothai, Thailand
http://www.blesele.org/

DSWT
David Sheldrick Wildlife Trust
Elephant Orphan Project
Dame Daphne Sheldrick
Nairobi, Africa
https://www.sheldrickwildlifetrust.org/

LEAP
Lucy's Edmonton Advocates' Project
Edmonton, Alberta, Canada
https://www.leapforlucy.com/

www.ingramcontent.com/pod-product-compliance
Lightning Source LLC
Chambersburg PA
CBHW072347270726
48659CB00023B/2430